Dorothy S. Gower

A gift from
Ruth Roberts
July '77

HAVE YOU HEARD

THE

CRICKET SONG

Have You Heard the Cricket Song

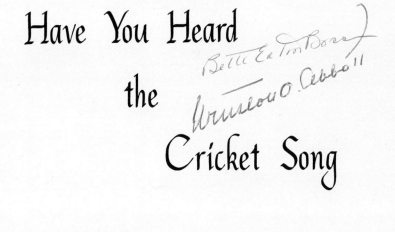

Words
WINSTON O. ABBOTT

Drawings
BETTE EATON BOSSEN

Published by
INSPIRATION HOUSE
South Windsor, Connecticut

This book is a companion volume to
COME CLIMB MY HILL
SING WITH THE WIND
and
COME WALK AMONG THE STARS

these words and drawings

are dedicated

to all whose hearts have

felt the weight of

a

falling

leaf

beauty gathered in the brightness of the sunny
  hours —

is often best remembered in the quiet dark —

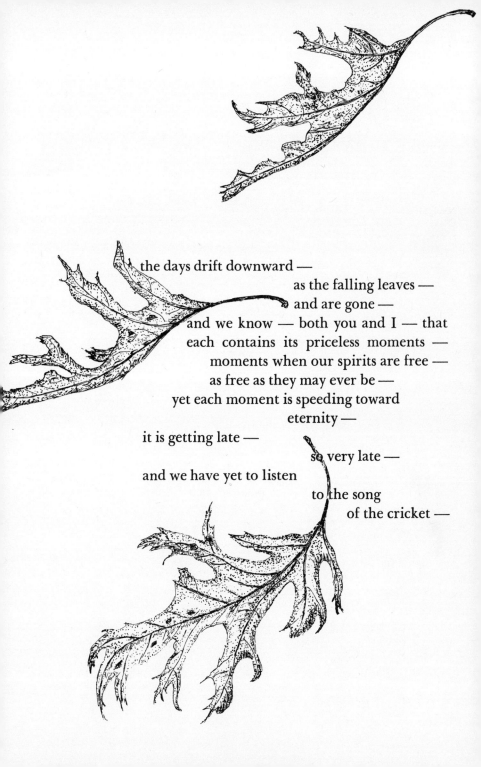

the days drift downward —
                    as the falling leaves —
                    and are gone —
            and we know — both you and I — that
            each contains its priceless moments —
                moments when our spirits are free —
                    as free as they may ever be —
            yet each moment is speeding toward
                            eternity —
        it is getting late —

                            so very late —

    and we have yet to listen

                        to the song
                            of the cricket —

one
　　lonely
　　　　night
　　　　　　I heard —

the hurrying footsteps
of the wind amid the
drying leaves —
and it was autumn —

and with patience — and impatience —

I waited through the
lingering hours of
darkness — while
the earth was still and sleeping —
and it was winter —

until
one
night
I heard —

the first faint trilling
    of the peepers
  in the frozen marshland — and
  it was spring —

to know life best —

        become a friend of the earth and
its living things — for the earth sustains your
life and mine —

        ever looking upward to the sunshine and
the rain — ever seeking beauty in the distant
stars — ever moving in life's mysterious circle
— ever portraying life's infallibility —

        the bursting seed —

        the fruit — the frost —

        and yet another seed —

become a friend of the patient and gentle
   earth —

        and you will understand
the meaning for your life — as I have come to
understand —

        the meaning for my own —

we have not wisdom
    until we know —
the sparrow and the thrush are one —
    and the dandelion becomes a rose —

peace would come to many troubled spirits —
                                  and healing
to many troubled hearts — and there would be
music everywhere — if each of us could have a
brook — where the clean water ripples over
shining pebbles — and goes on to eddy into little darkened pools where fish find shelter —
                        where lacy ferns nod to the
rhythm of the ever moving water — and the
songs of the thrush are heard in the cool green
shadows —

—

—

—

for the music of water is the music of life — and
each heart needs the sound of singing waters —
as each spirit needs a place of solitude —

                  where one
may hearken to the sounds that were born when
life was born — sounds that are elemental and
eternal — sounds once unknown to man —

                  for in that far distant
world where life began — man was not there to
listen —

if but once —
you have touched the hand
of the Creator —
there is music
in the croaking
of the frog —

there is so much of mystery in the
simplest thing — so much of beauty
in the commonplace —

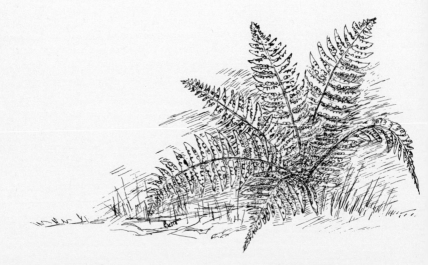

the shadows are not unfriendly —

                            as I once had
thought —

                because they are the deepest just
before the dark — and the dark was filled with
a fear of the untravelled and the unknown —
               but I have found — as the circling
years unfold — there is nothing of fear in the
darkness — unless it be its utter emptiness —
but this will never be — if love has touched
you with her gentleness —
the shadows are not unfriendly —

                            as I once had
thought —

                for I have found healing in the
midst of shadows — and love in the midst of
pain —

it is more than just a wall —

it is the toil of nameless hands more than a
hundred years ago — the skill and patience of
lives now unremembered and forgotten —

                                                yet the
wall remains — endowed with a legacy of
permanence — a thing of ever changing beauty
— embossed by time — with the viability of
life —

                           each stone etched with lichens —
soft gray in the warmth of sunlight — misty
green when the welcome rains come to wash the
meadow —

                              it is more than just a wall — this
heritage from those who have gone before —

                    what shall I leave
                        to those
                            who follow me —

these graceful trees —
                    hold something of my heart
upon their outstretched branches—for my hands
first pressed their scraggy roots into the warm
dark earth —
    and in return they have shared with me their
gifts of beauty — golden autumn leaves upon
their shining needles — the sparkle of winter
moonlight upon the burdening snow — new
and tender green in the miracle of spring —
fragrance in the dew-drenched summer morn-
ings —
                    —
              —
                    —

and now — after many years —
one has grown a little
nearer to the stars — and surely this was
meant to be — for in the golden sun-
shine of late afternoon — the shadow of
the taller reaches out to gently touch the
smaller —
and only because these trees have
shared their growth with me — do I
appreciate and understand —
that my life too has been gently touched
— and often — by the shadow of the
taller —
and for
this I shall be ever grateful —

one does not
need the
brilliant light
of galaxies afar —
if one
may have
the constant light
of just
a single
star —

in this hushed and shadowed wood — miracles
appear upon the forest floor — in gentle
pinks and burnished golds — in royal purple
and tangerine and lemon hues —

— life is being transmuted into life —
new life hidden deep within the sheltered woods
— yet brushed with all the fragile colors of the
sunset —

here the tired and weathered hands of the
Creator have found new strength — have
reached down into the moist and moulding
earth — to fashion new forms of life from the
residue of forgotten years — here the changeless
is ever changing — here yesterday mingles for
the moment with to-morrow —

if we rest for awhile in this quiet
place — we will share a sense of reverence for
the mystery of creation — and perhaps come to
understand that even the silence is filled with
sound —

listen —

that was the song
of the veery —

we call them weeds and pass them by —
   the goldenrod and thistle —
   the queen anne's lace and meadow rue —

these are the weeds —
      the common people of the earth —
the first to grow where man has scarred and
scorched the beauty of his heritage —
striving ever to erase the ugliness
that is man's thoughtlessness —
      these are the weeds —
      unwanted and disdained and trampled
      under foot —
            but friend of humming bird
            and bee
            and butterfly —

I have seen ten thousand
     migrant wings against the sky —
     but —
     yet to see one brush against
     another as they fly —

I remember —
how deep the snows —
how cold the winter winds —

do you remember
too —

there were no footsteps on this ancient shore
    when life was patterned for eternity
        beyond the tides a million years or
        more
            when life was cradled in the
            brooding sea —

yet when another million years had gone
    there were no markings on this lonely
    sand —
        no one to greet the coming of the dawn
        though life had made its way
        upon the land —

but sadly now — the sea has moved away
and left you to the storm — the wind —
the rain —
wait but a little while — until one day
the sea will come and take you
back again —

these we have loved —

these fragile fleeting things
that touch our hearts with
beauty —

and are gone —

let not this moment be of lessened beauty —
because one distant day — it may
remembered be —
with pain —

a life — a leaf —

a bursting bud upon the barren tree — the lonely crying of the wind — laughter of rain-drops — warmth of summer sun — and so many times the wrenching violence of storms —

and to some strangely chosen few — the song of a thrush from within the branches —

sometimes stars — sometimes sadness in the night — once an expectant rustling of the leaves — but the leaf must stay upon the branch until its autumn comes — fleeting days of glory — the chill of lonely nights — and finally freedom from the branch — time to drift unfettered on the wind — to embrace the earth where life began —

but for us this should not be a time of sorrow — for were we not chosen to hear the song of the thrush — you and I —

two lives — two leaves —

sometimes — sometimes a moment is greater
than eternity —
    that moment — when my faint and frightened
spirit is swept forward in the vast stream of
life —
          that moment — when every living thing
becomes a part of life — when life is truly
shared by every living thing —
                    that moment — when a
chickadee alights upon my outstretched hand —
friendly — unafraid — offering a song in return
for a seed —

              —

                 —

                    —

but in another moment — a fluttering
of busy wings —
                    and I am strangely
      apart and alone again — as empty
        and deserted as the nest upon
          the leafless branch —
                          but the
            chickadee will return upon
            another day — and I will be
              waiting with outstretched
                hand — as I have waited
                  countless times
                    before —

time

    cannot be measured

    in the presence of

        the stars —

the lights of infinity sparkle above the naked
branches — but you and I — mortals as we are
— have marked our foot prints on the freshly
fallen snow —
　　　　　but beauty such as this reaches across
both time and space to touch us with the
radiance of creation —
　　　　　let me reach out and take you by the
hand — that to-gether our earthbound spirits
may rise to meet the challenge of the stars —
　　　　　　　　　　　perhaps —
perhaps — in this one bright moment of
awareness — we shall come to know —
　　　　　　that these trees — and the stars
above them — and you and I — mortals as we
are — are but one in the wisdom of creation —

upon these gently rolling hills — and where the
great saltmarshes reach toward the sea — and
where the great winds sweep about the mountain
top —
    I have found these many things to fill the
needs of my spirit —
        strength —
                as the deep roots hold the tree
                against the storm —
      gentleness —
                as the summer breezes brush the
                ripening grain —
    A sense of sharing —
                as the sparrow feeds her
                helpless young —
                    —
                        —
                          —

courage —
     as the fragile snowdrop struggles
     from the frozen earth —
a sense of purpose —
     as the acorn ever holds the
     image of the oak —

faith —
 as the tiny seeds embark
 upon the wind —
and love —
 a love that is great enough
 to encompass all these
 things —
 for love
 is the essence
 of life —

each living thing has need of
other living things —
depends upon and is
depended upon —
and
hopefully
shares —

shade and shelter —
    food and fragrance —
      faith and friendship —
and often the need to learn that a gift is
not of lessened value if it is only a song —
    and of course you know that some of the
    living things are catalysts —
                    you did know
    that — didn't you — and it must ever be
    this way — for change is the order
    of life —

once I stood at dusk —
            waiting for the evening stars —
watching them grow ever brighter — needing the
peace that comes in the hush of a busy day —
            and I
shivered a little in the chill of the night —
and grieved that the Creator had granted me so
few years of life — so little time in which to
fill my heart with beauty —
            and a moth flew out
of the darkness — and fluttered about the
lantern — and I grieved even more that the
Creator had granted the moth but a half a
  moon —

— yet often with grief comes wisdom —

in every shaded wood —
in every sunlit field
and windswept meadow —
a
blossom
smiles
upon
the
world —

colored and fashioned according to its
needs of soil and sun —

and yet the most brightly
colored flowers — the most fragrant of blossoms
— live but a few brief hours or days —

for that is
the way it was meant to be — that each tiny
blossom must give back unto the earth — that
which it has taken from it —

even as you and I must give back to
life that which we have received from life —
and hopefully a little more —

for that too is the infinite
wisdom of creation —

why should we be afraid —

twilight is a time for sharing — and a time for remembering — sharing the fragrance of the cooling earth — the shadows of the gathering dusk —

here our two worlds meet and pass — the frantic sounds of man grow dimmer as the light recedes — the unhurried rhythm of the other world swells in volume as the darkness deepens —

it is not strange that discord has no place in this great symphony of sound —

it is not strange that a sense of peace descends upon all living things —

it is not strange that memories burn more brightly — as the things of substance lose their line and form in the softness of the dark —

—

—

—

twilight is a time for sharing — and a
time for remembering — remembering the things of
beauty wasted by our careless hands — our frequent
disregard of other living things — the many songs
unheard because we would not listen —
              listen to-night with all the
        wisdom of your spirit — listen too with
        all the compassion of your heart —
        lest there come another night —
          when there is only silence —

                                        a great
                                        and
                                        total
                                        silence —

a life — without love —
is a lonely bird
making its solitary way
above the lonely marsh —

it is written in sadness —
           that we often wish
           our lives to be
           small brooks —
           winding their casual
           way across the
           peaceful meadows —
when they were meant to be —
           great seas — whose
           smallest waves wash
           the distant shores
           of infinity —

come — let us walk into the sunset's glow —
into the dusty pink and golden sky —
and when we get there we will surely know
that love like beauty grows and cannot die —
and we will walk beyond these misted years
toward a dawn both beckoning and bright —

and not remember eyes once dimmed by tears
that fell unbidden in the lonely night —
come —